The Resume Queen's

Job Search Thesaurus

and

Career Guide

For Professionals

The Resume Queen's

Job Search Thesaurus
and
Career Guide

For Professionals

Joanne Meehl, M.S., IJCDC

 SATYA HOUSE PUBLICATIONS

Hardwick, Massachusetts

Satya House Publications
P. O. Box 122
Hardwick, Massachusetts 01037
www.satyahouse.com

First Edition

ISBN 978-0-9729191-3-5

Printed in the United States of America

For my clients, who teach me something vital every day.

Acknowledgments

My thanks go to my editor, Julie Murkette, whose sharp eye and suggestions were always right on.

Also, to Sandy Gochis, my invaluable Executive Assistant and unyielding researcher. Her insights and plain hard work in pulling all my notes together made this book possible.

And to David Balzotti, my resourceful business partner, wonderful husband, and relentless supporter and cheerleader.

Introduction

There are many good thesauri out there. However, they are for general use, and are big and fat. They are good for writers and others seeking alternative words, but too cumbersome for the job seeker.

The Resume Queen's Job Search Thesaurus and Career Guide is designed for professionals engaged in a job search. It's the first of its kind, designed to enhance your ability to "sell yourself" more effectively in comparison with your competitors.

Why I'm Sharing One of My Major Tools
I love words. I collect thesauri. I was frustrated, however, by having to wade through massive books of words or the thesaurus integrated into my word-processing software, to find just the words I needed for my clients' resumes. I began collecting my own terms, and eventually built a terrific little resource for myself.

Then I noticed how many clients complained of the inability to find "just a job search thesaurus." Finding the right word that conveys one's value, is a key part of each professional's job search. It just wasn't out there . . . until now.

Job Search Words

This thesaurus contains only words that are relevant for professionals in the job search, even beyond the resume. So you won't find eight synonyms for the word *snow*.

Now that still means a lot of words. But not so many that this book ends up being too big to carry to the library, career center or outplacement office, or too big to keep by your computer.

The focus is on words that define *action*.

. . . And Then Some

I've designed this book to be a companion during your job search. It's more than just a thesaurus. It's a guide to communicating during your job search . . . *to using words as tools*. Your job, during your job search, is to communicate your value to an employer. Without the ability to communicate effectively during this critical time, you won't get the job you want. Aren't you worth getting the job you *want*? That's even better than getting "a good job."

This book is organized in such a way that you'll find the words on the right-hand pages, from A to Z (actually W). On the opposite pages, you'll see *Quotes from the Queen* — tips about a particular word, tips about the job search, or thoughts about maintaining your motivation during the search.

So in these pages you'll find:

- Words (and phrases) and their synonyms

- Occasional narrative about the word or phrase: its pros, cons, best usage, when to avoid it, etc.

- Supportive material for the writing tasks of your job search, and help with various job search tools.

Source of the Words and Synonyms
After years of experience as a career coaching professional, career issues writer and essay writer, I have learned how the right language can help job candidates. I assembled a collection of words and then sought out other words from everyday American English.

What, No Marine Biology?
You'll notice that the words in this thesaurus are not field-specific. They don't focus on business or chemistry or child psychology. Each of those fields — and your field as well — has its own lexicon. You certainly know that collection of terms better than I do. Instead, this thesaurus helps you bridge the connection between what you've accomplished in your own work life and the mind of the decision-maker who's looking at your resume or the software that's screening it. Hiring managers take about 8-10 seconds to skim your resume before deciding if they want to read further. Make it as effective as you can so they read it, match you to the job, and then call you in for the interview.

About Key Words
This is a subject all its own. In short, companies generate lists of key words for each of their job categories. Some of the words are related to particular skills and experiences required for a particular job. Others are related to the type of person who would best fill the job. Still others come from the company culture, which can be found on their website and in their publications. All these key words are entered into a database. Then, the words in your resume are screened by software that looks for matches.

Think of your resume as a mini key word database. Your mini key word database must match the employer's bigger key word database in order to be "flagged" for an actual human being to read. Without such key words, your resume won't ever get read. Even when a company or organization has human screeners, key words are still important. That's how you make a connection between *you* and *them*.

My Beliefs

I have extensive experience in career choice counseling, career planning, and job search coaching. I share the following statements with my clients during a job search:

- Some lucky employer out there is looking for you. You just have to find them . . . and that takes work.

- You are worth it! Use tools that will work for you because you are worthy of getting the job YOU want.

These simple statements have great value. You might not recognize that now, but they're true. Believe in them, even if it's only on faith for the time being.

There are other such beliefs in these pages, all proven by the great things I've seen clients achieve over the years. If they help you, then it's made my day.

Your Ideas Will Help Others

As you use this book, you'll probably come up with some word ideas of your own. Please send your word ideas to: **Joanne@TheResumeQueen.com** for future editions! I can't promise that we'll use them, but I will send you a complimentary subscription to my newsletter, *Between the Trapezes*.

— Joanne Meehl

A

Ability
Aptitude, capability, capacity, command, competence, dexterity, expertise, faculty, intelligence, know-how, knowledge, power, proficiency, qualification, skill, strength, talent

Accelerate
Advance, build, drive, expedite, facilitate, forward, hasten, increase, move, progress, push, quicken, speed up

Accomplish(ed)
Verbs: Achieve, attain, carry through, carry out, complete, execute, finish, fulfill, gain, meet, produce, reach, realize, succeed

Adjectives: Able, adept, competent, experienced, proficient, qualified

Accurate
Careful, certain, conclusive, correct, definite, detailed, exact, factual, infallible, methodical, official, perfect, precise, specific

Achieve
Accomplish, acquire, actualize, attain, carry through, complete, conclude, earn, effect, execute, finish, fulfill, gain, hit, obtain, make, perform, produce, reach, realize

Acquire
Achieve, amass, assume, attain, earn, gain, incur, obtain, realize

Quotes From The Queen

Attitude. Whose attitude? Yours, and the person in the position to hire you. Yours, upbeat: "Here's what I can do for you." Theirs, 99% of the time: "I hope this is the person we hire! We have so much work piling up, and other managers are on my case to get it done. Please let this one be the one!"

A job seeker who "gets" both is far better equipped for the search and for the interview. And is more likely to land the job.

Adapt
Acclimate, accommodate, accustom, adjust, align, alter, change, comply, conform, fashion, fit, match, modify, prepare, readjust, revise, suit, tailor

Add
Annex, append, augment, bring, broaden, combine, complement, connect, contribute, enlarge, enrich, expand, fortify, heighten, increase, include, join, lend, supplement, total, unite, widen

Adept
Able, accomplished, capable, dexterous, effective, expert, experienced, good, polished, practiced, proficient, qualified, savvy, sharp, skilled, talented, versed

Administer
Administrate, apply, assign, conduct, control, direct, engineer, execute, govern, head, implement, lead, manage, officiate, operate, oversee, perform, preside, run, supervise

Advise
Caution, consult to, counsel, direct, guide, inform, instruct, notify, recommend, suggest, tutor

Advocate
Counsel, defend, promote, recommend, speak for, support, urge

Noun: counselor, champion

Allocate
Allot, apportion, appropriate, assign, budget, designate, distribute, grant, present, specify

Quotes From The Queen

Although we include *assist* here, it's passive and weak, so we don't recommend its use. Instead, use *"Member of team that revamped bidding process,"* or *"Key contributor who delivered necessary documentation."* It doesn't start with a verb, but it still does the job.

Analyze
Break down, consider, determine, dissect, evaluate, examine, figure, inspect, investigate, judge, resolve, review, scrutinize, study

Apply
Address, assign, dedicate, devote, direct, employ, focus, practice, put in motion, use

Appraise
Analyze, approximate, assay, assess, calculate, estimate, evaluate, examine, gauge, measure, price, rate, size, study, survey, valuate

Approve
Affirm, agree, authorize, back, certify, clear, commend, confirm, endorse, license, pass, permit, praise, recommend, sanction, support, uphold, validate

Arrange
Adapt, array, construct, devise distribute, draft fix, format, group, order, organize, plan, position, prepare, schedule, sort

Assemble
Call together, collect, compile, configure, congregate, construct, convene, create, erect, fashion, form, join, make, mold, produce, set up, shape, summon

Assess
Apprise, compute, consider, determine, evaluate, gauge, judge, measure, rate, review, survey, valuate, weigh

Assist
Aid, help, support

Attend to
Accompany, add(ed), augment, be present at

Quotes From The Queen

Blogs in your job search: If you have a personal blog, and you're using your real name, be careful to not post what you don't want read by a potential employer. Prospective employers will google your name more often than you know, so be sure everything there represents you in a professional manner. See *Portfolio* on page 70 for a better way to use the Internet for your job search.

B

Budget
Verbs: Allocate, allot, allow for, apportion, calculate, estimate, forecast, plan, schedule

Build/built
To make: Assemble, construct, compile, engineer, establish, fabricate, fashion, form, manufacture, produce

Bolster or strengthen: Actualize, augment, boost, create, expand, heighten, improve, perfect

Buy
Acquire, finance, obtain, procure, purchase, requisition, subsidize

Quotes From The Queen

A business card for your job search? Of course. First, if you're presently working for someone else, it's not ethical to use that business card. Also, you wouldn't want to use the card you have now because it doesn't represent you and your job search interests. Whether you're currently working for someone now or not, create a simple card *on good paper stock.* You can do this on your computer if you know how to use that feature and if you can find good paper. Or you can go to your local printer and order them. Black lettering on white stock is fine, listing your name, address, phone number(s), e-mail address, website if you have one, and your title and tagline. You can also list 2-3 phrases about yourself that quickly give the reader a good idea of what you can do.

C

Careful
Accurate, attentive, cautious, conscientious, deliberate, detailed, diligent, meticulous, mindful, observant, precise, prudent, scrupulous, thorough, thoughtful, vigilant, watchful

Centralize(d)
Assemble, center, concentrate, consolidate, contain, converge, focus, gather, streamline

Champion
Advocate, build

Noun: advocate

Change
Adjust, alter, convert, correct, diversify, modify, reconstruct, refashion, remodel, transfer, transform, turn, vary

Check
Approve, analyze, ascertain, compare, confirm, examine, inquire, inspect, investigate, monitor, review, study, survey, verify

Clarify
Define, delineate, elucidate, explain, illuminate, illustrate, interpret, simplify

Coach
Direct, educate, guide, instruct, mentor, prepare, prompt, ready, school, train

Quotes From The Queen

Career Research Meeting: Richard Nelson Bolles coined the term *informational interview* in the 1970s, and most people still call it this. However, because this approach of talking with people at target companies has been abused over the years *("I promise, I won't ask for a job, but can I bring you my resume?")*, I don't recommend using it. Because of that, and because the term *informational interview* really means an interview that's given as a courtesy to someone who may or may not be qualified for the job, I prefer the term *Career Research Meetings* — because that's really what they are.

This is a business conversation, preferably face-to-face, that addresses your career goals other than landing a job. I suggest people asking for such meetings NOT bring their resume, because doing so changes the purpose of the meeting from *research* to *job search*. A networking profile is a better tool in this situation. *(See more about this on page 58.)*

If, at the meeting, you are asked for your resume, you won't have it, so you'll have the opportunity to send it later. Better to use the resume to reconnect than to use it as an initial bludgeon.

Collaborate
Combine, concur, conspire, cooperate, cooperate with, co-produce, interface, participate, work jointly, work together, work with

Collate
Arrange, assemble, collect, compared, gather, integrate

Compare
Analyze, assimilate, collate, consider, contemplate, contrast, differentiate, discriminate, distinguish between, equate, examine, inspect, liken to, liken, match, study, weigh

Compile
Accumulate, amass, arrange, assemble, catalog, collect, compose, consolidate, gather, make, organize

Complete
Accomplish, achieve, actualize, close, conclude, consummate, end, execute, finalize, finish, fulfill, perform, realize

Compose
Author, compile, comprise, conceived, consists of, constitute, construct, create, design, fashion, forge, formed, invent, originate, produce

Compute
Calculate, count, determine, estimate, figured, measure, reckon

Conceive
Conception, conceptualize, contrive, create, design, devise, discover, envision, form a conception of, formulate, imagine, originate, realize, think, visualize

Quotes From The Queen

Contacts are the basis of your network. Make a list of contacts, starting with people you know well, then moving "outward" to people others know well, and so forth. When you're done with the first draft, you'll be pleasantly surprised to see dozens or even hundreds of names.

Conduct
Administer, arrange, chair, control, command, direct, engineer, govern, guide, handle, head, lead, manage, operate, orchestrate, organize, oversee, pilot, run, steer, supervise

Consolidate
Amalgamate, blend, centralize, coalesce, combine, compact, concentrate, integrate, join, meld, merge, streamline, strengthen, unify, unite

Construct
Build, create, design, devise, engineer, fabricate, formulate, manufacture, produce

Control
Administer, administrate, command, conduct, dictate, direct, dominate, govern, handle, instruct, lead, manage, operated, oversee, pilot, regulate, steer, supervise

Convert
Alter, change, metamorphose, modify, shift, transfigure, transform, translate, turn

Convey
Communicate, disclose, express, impart, pass on, project, put across, relate, transmit

Cooperate
Aid, assist, collaborate, coordinate, interface, participate, partner

Coordinate
Accommodate, adapt, adjust, align, arrange, attune, balance, combine, harmonize, integrate, organize, plan, proportion, reconcile, schedule, set up

Quotes From The Queen

Conduct is a good word, but can be too broad at times. *"Conducted training session"* means what? Instead, say *"Lead training session,"* if that's what you did, or *"Created training materials."* It gets to the point and it better portrays what you really did.

Counsel
Verbs: Advise, advocate, consult, direct, encourage, guide, inform, instructed, recommend, prompt, suggest

Create
Author, build, cause, compose, conceive, contrive, design, develop, establish, fabricate, form, formulated, found, generate, initiate, institute, invent, make, organize, originate, plan, produce, set up, shape, start, visualize

Creative
Adept, artistic, imaginative, innovative, inspired, inventive, original, resourceful, skillful, talented

Cut
Abate, abbreviate, abridge, clip, condense, curtail, decrease, delete, eliminate, lessen lower, pare, reduce, shorten, slash, trim, truncate

Quotes From The Queen

Cover Letters are still read and sought after by employers because they display the candidate's ability to write, beyond the resume, which may have been written by someone else. Today, however, they more likely take the form of e-mail instead of hard copy or as an attachment to an e-mail.

Cover letters should be customized for *that* job at *that* employer. Each letter should make four key points:

1. Tell them where you saw the posting and that you're interested.

2. Tell them why you want to work for *them*.

3. Match your relevant skills and talents to the requirements of the job.

4. Call for action (ask for the interview).

D

Decide
Agree, conclude, determine, elect, establish, figure, judge, resolve, rule, select, settle, surmise, weigh

Delegate
Appoint, ascribe, assign, authorize, cast, charge, choose, commission, consign, depute, designate, elect, empower, license, mandate, name, relegate, select, transfer

Deliver
Administer, allot, bring, convey, dispense, distribute, give, impart, pass, provide, remit, supply, transfer, transmit, turn over

Demonstrate
Delineate, describe, display, exhibit, explain, evince, illustrate, present, prove, show

Design
Verbs: Arrange, blueprint, conceive, conceptualize, construct, contrive, create, delineate, develop, devise, draft, fabricate, fashion, form, formulate, frame, intend, invent, originate, plan, produce, propose

Determine(d)
Verbs: Ascertain, conclude, decide, establish, figure, judge, resolve, rule

Adjectives: Ambitious, decisive, driven, intent, persistent, resolute, serious

Quotes From The Queen

Descriptive words in your resume: Otherwise known as adjectives and adverbs, *carefully used*, these can bring life and color to your resume. I advocate the judicious use of them. If you overuse them by putting *"Successful. . . ,"* for example, in every bulleted item in your resume, it would soon lose all meaning. The best approach is to point out the successful result of your actions. For example, instead of saying *"Strong production skills,"* say *"Cut production time by 34%."*

Develop
Advance, create, cultivate, elaborate, enlarge, enrich, establish, expand, form, formulate, generate, heighten, improve, institute, mature, organize, originate, produce, promote

Devise
Arrange, blueprint, cast, chart, conceive, conceptualize, construct, contrive, craft, create, design, discover, draft, fabricate, fashion, form, formulate, imagine, invent, make, originate, plan, plot, prepare, shape

Diagnose
Analyze, canvas, determinate, distinguish, examine, finger, identify, interpret, investigate, pinpoint, study

Direct
Administer, advise, aim, command, conduct, control, counsel, define, govern, guide, head, influence, instruct, lead, manage, operate, order, oversee, pilot, regulate, rule, show, steer, supervise, teach

Disciplined
Adjectives: Accomplished, efficient, practiced, trained

Discover
Ascertain, detect, determine, discern, disclose, encounter, expose, find, identify, invent, learn, notice, observe, recognize, reveal, uncover, unearth, unmask

Distribute
Administer, allocate, allot, apportion, appropriate, assign, bestow, circulate, consign, dealt, disburse, dispense, disseminate, issue, parcel, sort, spread

Quotes From The Queen

You'll see that the word *duties* isn't here. It's a word that says *"things I* had *to do,"* and that's not the attitude you want to convey. Plus, it's descriptive and not about results and accomplishments. And job search is all about communicating your *accomplishments.*

Diversified
Assorted, different, disparate, divergent, miscellaneous, several, varied, various, wide-ranging

Divert
Alter, avert, change, deflect, detour, deviate, modify, rechannel, redirect, reorient, turn

Document
Verbs: Chronicle, enter, file, inscribe, record, register

Double
Amplify, augment, copy, duplicate, enlarge, grow, increase, magnify, multiply, pair, repeat, two-fold

Drive
Actuate, boost, compel, encourage, force, impel, induce, inspire, mobilize, move, press, prompt, propel, push, stimulate, thrust, urge

Duplicate
Copy, double, dualize, repeat, replicate, reproduce, second

Quotes From The Queen

What's your *elevator speech?* It's your 30-second (or 60-second or 2-minute) commercial. It's what you say in response to the question, *"Tell me about yourself."* It's called an elevator speech — despite the fact that people seldom talk in elevators — because it's supposed to be short enough to say while on a brief elevator ride. It should address your value and what you bring to the job; it is not your career history or personal biography.

E

Earn
Achieve, acquire, attain, collect, deserve, gain, merit, obtain, procure, rate, realize, reap, receive

Edit
Adapt, alter, amend, analyze, arrange, check, censor, collect, correct, draft, finish, modify, polish, prep, recalibrate, refine, revise, rewrite, select, style, tighten

Eliminate
Cancel, delete, disqualify, eradicate, exclude, liquidate, remove, suspend, waive

Encourage
Advocate, back, boost, embolden, fortify, galvanize, hearten, incite, impel, inspire, inspirit, promote, rally, sponsor, stimulate, stir, strengthen, support

Energetic
Active, driving, dynamic, enterprising, fresh, industrious, lively, spirited, tireless, vibrant, vigorous

Ensure
Ascertain, assure, certify, confirm, guarantee, make certain

Establish
Charter, constitute, create, effect, enact, endow, entrench, formulate, found, incorporate, install, institute, launch, organize, originate, place, plant, provide, sanction, start

Quotes From The Queen

E-mail address: for job search, this should be professional in nature. In other words, it shouldn't be cute or tacky or risqué.

Estimate
Verbs: Appraise, approximate, assess, budget, calculate, compute, conclude, determine, evaluate, figure, forecast, gauge, guess, judge, measure, predict, rate, surmise

Evaluate
Appraise, ascertain, assay, assess, determine, estimate, examine, gauge, judge, measure, rank, rate, survey, weigh

Expand
Amplify, augment, balloon, bolster, broaden, develop, enlarge, extend, flourish, grow, increase, inflate, intensify, magnify, maximize, outspread, spread

Expedite
Accelerate, advance, aid, assist, boost, drive, enable, facilitate, forward, further, hasten, help, promote, quicken, rush, speed

Experience
Nouns: Background, education, knowledge, practice, skill, understanding

Experienced
Adjectives: Able, accomplished, capable, competent, expert, knowledgeable, masterful, practiced, proficient, qualified, rounded, seasoned, skillful, trained

Quotes From The Queen

E-mail signature: this is your name at the end of an e-mail, inserted automatically by your e-mail program if you designate it as such. It should contain your full name, your tagline, your phone number(s), your e-mail address, and your URL if you have a website. Why your e-mail address, even though it's being sent by you at your e-mail address? So that the recipient can copy all your pertinent information into their electronic mail directory or address book.

F

Facilitate
Advance, aid, assist, ease, expedite, further, help, promote, simplify, speed, support

Field
Area, avocation, bounds, discipline, domain, environment, expertise, occupation, realm, specialty, sphere, study, territory, vocation

Finalize
Complete, conclude, decide, end, finish, settle

Finance
Back, capitalize, endow, found, fund, promote, sponsor, subsidize, support, underwrite

Flexible
Adaptable, affable, amenable, compliant, cooperative, formative, manageable, open, receptive, resilient, responsive, versatile

Forecast
Verbs: Anticipate, augur, calculate, estimate, determine, figure, gauge, plan, predetermine, predict, project, reason, surmise

Quotes From The Queen

Exit statement: This is the answer to the question *"Why did you leave your last job?"* or *"Why are you leaving your current job?"* Keep your answer short and simple. My observation is the longer your answer, the greater your chances of it devolving into a defensive statement on your part. Practice your answer so that it comes out comfortably. Do not sound angry or defensive no matter what the reason for having left. In fact, you should try to add something positive in your statements such as *"It was the right business decision for the health of the company."*

Resist the urge to elaborate and make it more complicated. Here's an example of a short and simple exit statement:

"The X Corporation bought our company and shut down our division, thus eliminating several positions including mine, which really was necessary for the company's direction now. However, they kept me on as a contractor for a few months after that, because they were pleased with my work. I believe I can bring that same level of flexibility and excellence here."

Formulate
Compose, contrive, create, design, develop, devise, draft, invent, originate, plan, prepare

Found
Begin, commence, create, erect, establish, form, initiate, institute, launch, organize, start

Furnish
Afford, endow, equip, outfit, provide, supply

Quotes From The Queen

What does the greeting on **your phone's voice mail** or answering machine sound like? Is it short? Friendly yet professional? Useful? During a job search, it's not the time to have a greeting done by your toddler, or to use coarse language, or to display an attitude. So listen to your greeting with an employer's ear and re-do it if necessary.

G

Gain
Verbs: Accomplish, achieve, acquire, add, advance, attain, augment, benefit, earn, increase, obtain, procure, reach, realize, reap

Generate
Create, develop, devise, effect, fabricate, form, initiate, institute, introduce, make, originate, produce, yield

Guide
Verbs: Advise, channel, conduct, control, counsel, direct, educate, handle, head, instruct, lead, manage, navigate, oversee, point, show, steer, supervise, usher

Quotes From The Queen

Honesty on a resume and in presenting yourself throughout your job search is an absolute must. Not only is this the ethical way to present yourself, but once you are hired, your resume becomes a legal document. Lies or semi-truths in a resume can become very public grounds for getting fired, even years later and even if you are a star performer.

H

Handle
Administer, command, conduct, control, deal, direct, execute, guide, head, manage, maneuver, operate, oversee, run, supervise, transact

Head
Administer, captain, command, control, direct, govern, guide, lead, manage, oversee, regulate, run, steer, supervise

Help
Advance, aid, assist, benefit, boost, contribute, cooperate, encourage, enhance, facilitate, further, improve, promote, support

Quotes From The Queen

Informational interview: This is what's commonly known as the name for the meeting you get with someone in your network in order to learn more about a company or possible job. I call them *career research meetings* instead, so see *Career Research Meetings* on page 24. It's the best way to tap the "hidden" (really, unadvertised) job market.

I

Identify
Analyze, certify, classify, determine, diagnose, discern, discover, distinguish, establish, found, label, name, pinpoint, select

Imaginative
Artistic, clever, constructive, creative, enterprising, ingenious, inspired, inventive, originative, resourceful

Implement
Actualize, apply, bring about, carry out, effect, employ, enable, execute, invoke, perform, start

Improve
Advance, ameliorate, augment, better, boost, develop, elevate, embellish, enhance, enrich, increase, lift, perfect, polish, refine, renew, revive, sharpen, strengthen, update, upgrade

Improvise
Brainstorm, compose, concoct, contrive, devise, extemporize, fabricate, invent

Increase
Verbs: Accrue, accumulate, advance, aggrandize, amplify, augment, boost, broaden, build, climb, compound, deepen, develop, elevate, enhance, enlarge, expand, extend, further, gain, grow, heighten, intensify, magnify, mount, multiply, raise, sharpen, strengthen, supplement, widen

Quotes From The Queen

Key words: Think of your resume not only as a marketing document, but as a miniature database of key words. At large organizations, your resume is incorporated into their resume bank for that opening or a future one. Then the hiring manager or HR gives a list of key words for that job, and looks for resumes that make the best match. Those are the resumes that finally get looked at by human eyes.

Influence
Nouns: Authority, character, clout, command, credit, jurisdiction, importance, inspiration, leadership, power, predominance, prominence, reputation, strength, weight

Verbs: affect, alter, change, control, convert, effect, guide, impel, impress, lead, persuade, sway

Initiate
Begin, cause, commence, establish, install, institute, introduce, facilitate, launch, open, organize, originate, pioneer, propose, start

Innovate
Change, introduce, modify, pioneer, reform

Inspect
Appraise, assess, audit, check, evaluate, examine, investigate, observe, probe, question, review, scan, scrutinize, search, study, survey

Inspire
Affect, drive, embolden, guide, impel, influence, motivate, spur, urge

Install
Establish, furnish, initiate, institute, introduce, place, plant, set up

Institute
Begin, commence, create, develop, enact, establish, form, found, initiate, introduce, launch, open, pioneer, start

Instruct
Acquaint, advise, brief, coach, command, counsel, direct, educate, guide, inform, lead, lecture, mentor, order, prepare, school teach, train

Quotes From The Queen

Generate a *list of key words* and phrases that you can swap in and out of your resume. Suppose you are a Product Manager, but you've also been a Program Manager, and are still qualified to do both. A handy tool for you would be the list of key words that will work for one, and another list that works for the other. That way you have a *key word bank* to go to when there's an opening and you'll save yourself a lot of effort and time while customizing your resume.

Instrumental
Key, important, vital, critical

Integrate
Accommodate, amalgamate, assimilate, attune, blend, combine, compact, consolidate, coordinate, fuse, harmonize, incorporate, intersperse, join, link, merge, mingle, mix, unite

Interpret
Clarify, construe, define, delineate, describe, explain, illustrate, translate, understand

Interview
Nouns: Conference, consultation, meeting

Verbs: Confer, consult, converse, evaluate, probe, question

Introduce
Make known: Acquaint, announce, inform, present, propose

To begin: Commence, enter, establish, found, inaugurate, induct, initiate, insert, install, institute, interpolate, launch, present, submit

Invent
Author, compose, conceive, construct, contrive, create, design, devise, discover, fashion, forge, formulate, found, originate, patent, produce

Investigate
Analyze, check, examine, explore, inspect, inquire, probe, research, review, search, study

Quotes From The Queen

Motivation during the job search is critical to your success. One of my favorite things to say to job seekers is "There are no cat skeletons in trees." This is usually met with a quizzical look. So I explain: There are no cat skeletons in trees because eventually they *do* come down. In the same way, you will get a job. So have faith that even if it takes longer than you'd like, you *will* get a job . . . a better job! Sometimes moments of faith like this, whether from these statements or your own, can fan the flames of motivation.

J

Judgment
Reasoning, decision-making, understanding, wisdom, rationale, logic, intuition, sense, good sense, prudence

Judicious
Accountable, astute, careful, diplomatic, discerning, discriminating, measured, prudent, rational, reasonable, responsible, thoughtful, trustworthy, wise

Juggle
Multitask, balance, manage, organize, deal with, fit in

Quotes From The Queen

There's nothing mysterious about *networking*: it's just talking to and *listening* to people you know and people they know. If you "ask around" about the best dentist in town or a good hair stylist, and you get information that way, that's networking. It's the same when it comes to your career. Talk to people you know, listen to their ideas and their information, and you will expand your network.

It's been said that we each have 250 people in our active network. When you attend a networking meeting, especially one related to job search, someone in the room may very well know the hiring manager in a target company of yours. Asking for and providing information is the heart of networking.

K

Key
Basic, central, chief, crucial, critical, essential, fundamental, instrumental, important, leading, main, major, pivotal primary, principal, significant, vital

Knowledge
Ability, aptitude, awareness, comprehension, expertise, familiarity, grasp, mind, practice

Quotes From The Queen

Networking Profile: This is a one-page synopsis of your career for *networking* purposes. It is meant for your networking contacts, not for employers. The goal of a networking profile is to give enough information about you so that the networking contact can help and/or refer you on to others who can help. Like your resume, you state your contact information and include a *Professional Summary* like the one on your resume (it may even be identical). Because networking profiles are more broad-brushed than resumes with their detailed bullets, here you should include statements about your skills, your competencies, and your successes. List the companies where you've worked, along with your titles, and end it with a list of target companies. Called *Executive Profiles* by some, for more senior managers.

See **Professional Summary** on page 72 for more information about that part of a resume. See **Target Companies** on page 88 for more about that aspect of the job search.

L

Launch
Begin, commence, establish, found, initiate, institute, introduce, open, propel, start

Lead
Guide: Captain, conduct, drive, escort, handle, head, manage, pilot, regulate, steer, supervise

Influence: Advise, cause, direct, govern, persuade, spearhead, supervise

Learn(ed)
Verbs: Acquire, ascertain, attain, determine, discover, master, unearth

Adjectives: Academic, accomplished, experienced, knowledgeable, practiced, proficient, skilled, versed

Lower
Abate, curtail, decrease, deflate, diminish, downsize, drop, minimize, reduce, shave, slash

Quotes From The Queen

Numerals: Just about every writing guide out there says the writer must spell out a number under 10 (zero, one, two . . .), and may use the numeral itself for numbers 10 or over. I usually break that rule because the appearance of a numeral on a resume (0, 1, 2 . . .) is more eye-catching (to both humans and screening software) than the number spelled out.

M

Maintain
Continue, control, manage, perpetuate, preserve, proceed, retain, support, sustain, uphold

Manage
Administer, command, conduct, control, counsel, direct, engineer, govern, guide, handle, head, instruct, lead, maintain, officiate, operate, oversee, preside, regulate, steer, supervise

Market
Advertise, deal, dispense, exchange, furnish, merchandise, offer, package, retail, sell, trade, vend

Mathematical
Analytical, computative, exact, precise, scientific

Mediate
Arbitrate, broker, intercede, moderate, negotiate, reconcile, resolve

Merge
Amalgamate, assimilate, blend, centralize, combine, concentrate, consolidate, converge, fuse, incorporate, integrate, intermingle, join, meld, mingle, mix, unify, unite

Modernize
Better, develop, improve, redesign, redevelop, refresh, regenerate, rejuvenate, remake, remodel, renew, renovate, revamp, revive, update

Quotes From The Queen

Online job search: Compare today's job search with one done in 1987 or 1997, and you'll see a vast difference. The Internet has revolutionized the search. For example, today most companies won't look at faxed or mailed resumes, only those that are e-mailed, because their databases are set up for that method only.

A word of caution about using the Net: attempting to do a job search at your keyboard, without actually going to meetings or networking groups, will just about guarantee you a long, frustrating job search, or a job that you didn't really want but that "was available."

Modify
Adapt, adjust, alter, change, convert, correct, edit, innovate, recast, refashion, reform, reorganize, reshape, revise, rework, shift, temper, transform, vary

Monitor
Audit, check, follow, observe, oversee, supervise, track, watch

Motivate
Activate, cause, drive, excite, fire, galvanize, impel, incline, induce, inspire, inspirit, move, persuade, pique, prompt, propel, rouse, spark, spur, stimulate

Multilingual
Linguist, polyglot

Multitask
Juggle, balance

Quotes From The Queen

Over 40? Be careful with your language. Be sure to use the language used in your field today: *IT* instead of *MIS*, or *MIS* instead of *Data Processing*, for example. Avoid these phrases when interviewing: *"When I was your age,"* or *"In my day. . . ."* or *"That's how we did it 30 years ago."* You want the focus on *what you can do*, not on your age, and if you sound like you're obsessed with your age, they'll wonder if you can do the job.

N

Negotiate
Accommodate, adjust, agree, arbitrate, arrange, bargain, compose, compromise, concert, confer, contract, deal, debate, discuss, intermediate, mediate, settle, transact

Network
Verbs: communicate, connect, interact, to find connections, establish conections, talk with others, exchange information

Nouns: contacts, connections, peers, associations, system of connections, people one knows

Notable
Outstanding, high profile, important, noteworthy, rare, well-known, serious, unique

Numerous
Plentiful, many

Quotes From The Queen

You don't see *oversee* or *oversaw* in this book, because *manage* and *direct* are better and more to the point about what you did. *Oversaw* is weak and means "watch over." It does not pass the "So what?" test on your resume. If you *supervised* or *managed* something, then those are the words to use.

O

Observe
Obey: Adhere, comply, conform, follow, honor

Watch: Detect, discern, discover, follow, monitor, note, notice, perceive, saw, study, survey, view

Obtain
Access, accomplish, achieve, acquire, attain, collect, earn, gain, gather, get, procure, reach, realize, reap, secure, take

Open
Begin, commence, exhibit, expand, initiate, launch, spread, start, unbar, unfold

Operate
Administer, conduct, control, direct, drive, effectuate, engineer, function, handle, head, lead, manage, maneuver, perform, run, steer, work

Opportunity
Chance, moment, occasion, possibility, potential

Organize
Found: Build, construct, create, design, establish, fashion, form, institute, mastermind, mobilize, plan, shape, start

Order: Arrange, catalog, classify, coordinate, group, methodize, rank, regulate, structure, systemize, tailor

Quotes From The Queen

PDFs (Portable Document Format files) are valuable tools in the world of business because they can be accessed by all computers, aren't easy to change, and because the file size can be reduced, which makes them easier to send over the Internet. But *DO NOT* use them in your job search, especially for your resume! This is because most companies' screening methods are set up for Microsoft® Word only, and because recruiters will want to take your resume and make changes to it that fit their style. Sending a PDF is likely to mean your resume won't even get entered into a company's database, much less looked at by anyone there.

Originate
Begin, compose, conceive, create, derive, design, develop, discover, draft, evolve, fashion, form, found, generate, initiate, innovate, institute, introduce, invent, launch, pioneer, produce, start

Overhaul
Audit, check, debug, fix, improve, inspect, mend, rebuild, recondition, reexamine, regenerate, reconstruct, renew, repair, restore, revamp, survey

Quotes From The Queen

Portfolio: In many cases, having a portfolio, whether in hard copy in a nice binder that you bring with you to interviews, or online, can help you in your job search. It's a collection of some of your best work, excellent reviews, letters of thanks, and so forth. This supports what you say in your resume with real-life examples. Costs can range from less than $20 for the paper version to $2,000 or more for the online type, which can get elaborate (sound files, video, etc.). If you know how to create a website, you can easily create an online version yourself.

P

Perform
Accomplish, achieve, complete, effect, execute, finish, fulfill, function, meet, operate, realize

Persuade
Affect, assure, cajole, coax, convert, convince, counsel, exhort, induce, influence, lead, prompt, reason, sway, urge

Plan
Verbs: Arrange, blueprint, calculate, cast, chart, craft, design, develop, devise, engineer, fabricate, form, formulate, frame, map, organize, outline, plot, prepare, project, schedule, shape, strategize

Prepare
Arrange, assemble, condition, develop, equip, fix, formulate, make, plan, qualify, ready

Present
Acquaint, cite, demonstrate, display, exhibit, give, introduce, manifest, offer, pitch, proffer, show, submit

Prioritize
Arrange, grade, order, place, rank, rate, schedule

Process
Verbs: Administer, analyze, handle, manage, prepare, treat

Quotes From The Queen

Professional Summary: This is the part of the resume right under your title, near the top of the first page. It describes you as a professional, regardless of your field. Here are a couple of examples:

Customer-driven Operations Executive with ROI focus. Dynamic, creative, forward-thinking team player. Intuitive problem solver skilled in leading multiple departments with complex projects while meeting revenue goals. Proven business acumen with outstanding impact on sales. Energetic, with track record as catalyst for growth.

Customer Service professional with strong sense of classic style. Friendly, diplomatic, energetic, organized, and efficient. Goal-oriented and self-motivated. Multitasks well, graceful under pressure. Readily assesses client's needs. Strong awareness of current trends. Management potential.

A good career coach can help you come up with one that fits you. I recommend using a summary because they tell a potential employer who you are. After all, people hire *people*, not resumes.

Produce
Assemble, build, compose, construct, create, deliver, design, develop, fabricate, form, generate, invent, manufacture, originate, yield

Program
Verbs: Arrange, book, calculate, compute, control, design, figure, organize, plan, process, schedule, slate

Promote
Advance, aid, ascent, assist, back, better, bolster, boost, champion, elevate, encourage, endorse, forward, foster, further, graduate, help, hype, improve, launch, publicize, push, raise, recommend, sponsor, support, urge, upgrade

Propose
Advocate, assert, broach, introduce, offer, pose, present, proffer, recommend, solicit, suggest, submit, tender

Provide
Afford, bestow, endow, equip, fit, furnish, grant, outfit, supply, support

Purchase
Acquire, acquisition, attain, buy, earn, gain, get, invest, obtain, procure, realize, select

Quotes From The Queen

References available upon request is not needed on a resume. It just takes up valuable space you can use for something else that better sells you. It's *assumed* that you have references an employer can contact. Your references are *not* part of your resume. Instead, they belong as a separate document. Have three or four, and these should be a mix: a former or current manager, a peer or colleague who knows your work, perhaps a customer or someone who reported to you. You should have their name, phone number, and e-mail address for ease of contact, though they will most likely receive a phone call. Also vital: a brief phrase that describes who they are to you. *"Former manager while at Johnson, Inc."* is plenty.

Q

Qualified
Adjectives: Able, accomplished, adept, capable, certified, competent, disciplined, efficient, eligible, equipped, experienced, expert, instructed, knowledgeable, licensed, practiced, proficient, proved, skilled, skillful, suitable, suited, tested, trained, versed

Quality
Ability, aspect, attribute, element, factor, features, traits

Quotes From The Queen

Coach your references! This means, they will appreciate your reminding them of the various projects you and they worked on together, and what you did to make them successful. Ensure that each of them says something substantial about you AND says something *different* than the other references will say about you. It's nice if all of them say you're a hard worker, but not as effective as if each says something important about you. So one may emphasize your ability to lead teams, while another may focus instead on how well you use limited resources. Another may be able to address your strengths *and* your main weakness, neutralizing the latter so that you don't have to. Doing this gives you a more well-rounded standing with the prospective employer.

R

Raise

Verbs: Advance, amplify, augment, boost, elevate, grew, heighten, hike, increase, inflate, lift, promote, rise, uplift

Receive

Accept, acquire, admit, assume, collect, gain, get, incur, inherit, obtain, redeem, secure, take

Recommend

Acclaim, advise, advocate, applaud, approve, celebrate, commend, endorse, praise, prize, propose, sanction, suggest, support, urge

Record

Catalog, chronicle, document, enter, enumerate, file, indicate, list, log, maintain, mark, note, register, report, tabulate, written

Recruit

Engage, enlist, enroll, enter, gather, got, induct, obtain, procure, select

Redesign

Change, engineer, improve, refresh, regenerate, revise, revive

Reduce

Abate, abbreviate, abridge, clip, condense, consolidate, curtail, cut, decrease, dilute, diminish, downgrade, lessen, limit, lower, minimize, pare, restrict, shave, shorten, slash, taper, trim

Quotes From The Queen

"Responsible for. . . ." **Do not use this phrase!** That's why you don't see it here. It's a phrase that's passive. If you *managed* something, say so. If you were asked to do something, talk about how you were *selected* to do this, *recruited* to do it. Otherwise you sound like a reluctant parent.

Refine
Better, clarify, enhance, hone, improve, perfect, polish, smooth

Relate(d)
Verbs: Chronicle, describe, narrate, recount, report, state, tell

Adjectives: Affiliate, ally, associate, cognate, complementary, concern, connect, correlative, correspond, interconnect, kindred, link, pertain, pertinent, relevant

Reliable
Conscientious, devoted, established, honest, positive, proved, reputable, respectable, responsible, sincere, solid, sound stable, steady, trustworthy

Reorganize
Change, improve, readjust, rearrange, reconstruct, regroup, reorder, revise

Repair
Correct, fix, mend, overhaul, rebuild, recondition, rectify, refurbish, remedy, renovate, restore, revamp, service

Report
Account, announce, broadcast, communicate, declare, describe, disclose, document, inform, note, notify, present, publish, record, relate, state

Represent
Act for, delineate, denote, depict, epitomize, exemplify, personify, picture, portray, serve, steward, symbolize, typify

Research
Verbs: Analyze, delve, examine, explore, investigate, probe, search, scrutinize, study

Nouns: Analysis, assessment, examination, inquiry, review

Quotes From The Queen

What is the resume's job? It's to get you *the interview*. So it's not an accounting of every single job you've had or every course you've taken, but instead it's a marketing document. That means it focuses on what's relevant to your career goal.

Resolve
Verbs: Analyze, answer, clear, conclude, decide, determine, decipher, discern, dispel, establish, figure, fix, settle, unravel

Nouns: Character, drive

Responsibility
Accountability, authority, capabilities, care, charge, commitments, contract, duty, jurisdiction, liability, obligation, requirement

Responsible
Accountable, capable, competent, conscientious, creditable, effective, efficient, judicious, qualified, sensible, stable, sound, steady, trustworthy

Restore
Improve, rebuild, reconstruct, recover, reestablish, regain, reinstate, rejuvenate, renew, repair, replace, return, revive

Retrieve
Recapture, reclaim, recoup, recuperate, recover, regain

Review
Verbs: Analyze, assess, check, critique, edit, evaluate, examine, inspect, interpret, judge, reconsider, reevaluate, scrutinize, study, survey, weigh

Revise
Alter, amend, change, correct, edit, improve, modify, perfect, polish, redraft, reorganize, restyle, retool, revamp, rework, rewrite, tighten, update, upgrade

Quotes From The Queen

The "So What?" Test: Does every bullet on your resume pass the *"So What?"* test? In other words, does it address some aspect of your value to an employer? Or does it just make a statement to which we can say *"Well, so what?"* For more on this, see *Value* on page 92.

S

Schedule
Arrange, book, engineer, organize, plan, plot, record, register, slate

Select
Choose, cull, decide, determine, elect, name, opt, pick, prefer

Sell
Auction, close, deal, give, liquidate, market, merchandise, retail, supply, trade, vend, wholesale

Serve
Act, aid, assist, attend, foster, fulfill, function, handle, help, officiate, promote, work

Service
Aid, assist, help, maintain, sustain

Set up
Arrange, assemble, began, construct, create, erect, establish, found, inaugurate, institute, open, prearrange, prepare, start

Show
Convince, demonstrate, direct, display, exhibit, explain, guide, illustrate, inform, instruct, lead, note, present, reveal, tell

Simplify
Abridge, clarify, clear, condense, explain, interpret, shorten, streamline, uncomplicate

Solve
Answer, calculate, clarify, decipher, decode, determine, elucidate, explain, figure, fix, reason, resolve, settle, unfold, unlock, unravel, untangle, work

Sort
Arrange, catalogue, categorize, class, classify, file, grade, group, index, list, order, rank, screen, type

Spark
Activate, excite, incite, initiate, inspire, kindle, start, stimulate, trigger

Spearhead
Begin, chair, command, direct, head, lead, marshal, mastermind, organize, pioneer, start, steer

Staff
Verbs: Employ, supply

Standardize
Assimilate, institutionalize, normalize, order, regiment, regulate, systemize

Start
Activate, begin, commence, create, embark, establish, found, implement, inaugurate, initiate, institute, introduce, issue, launch, lead, open, organize, originate, pioneer

Streamline
Abridge, align, centralize, compact, concentrate, consolidate, contour, organize, reduce, simplify

Strengthen
Add, bolster, brace, empower, energize enhance, fortify, heighten, increase, intensify, reinforce, secure, sharpen, stabilize, substantiate, support, tone, vitalize

Structured
Adjectives: Arranged, disciplined, formed, logical, methodic, methodical, ordered, organized, precise, systematic

Study(ied)
Verbs: Analyze, calculate, consider, contemplate, deliberate, examine, inspect, research, survey

Adjectives: Intentional, knowledgeable, purposeful, thoughtful, thought-out

Succeed
Accomplish, achieve, arrive, attain, earn, ensue, flourish, follow, fulfill, conclude, realize, reach, reach the goal

Success(ful)
Fortunate, lucrative, noteworthy, outstanding, productive, profitable, prosperous, rewarding, strong, thriving

Summarize
Abridge, condense, encapsulate, recap, restate, review, summate, synopsize

Supersede
Countermand, follow, invalidate, override, overrule, overturn, replace, supplant, usurp

Supervise
Administer, advise, conduct, control, direct, guide, handle, head, manage, overlook, oversee, regulate, run, steer, superintend

Quotes From The Queen

Taglines are simply short, catchy statements about who you are and what you do, so that it's easier to explain your value when you're talking with a potential employer or when you're networking. One of my clients, Mike, dubbed himself *"The Geek Who Can Speak"* because as technical as he was, he could also do marketing and sales, not a common combination of skills. For anyone who meets him and who cannot remember his name, as soon as you say, "You know him; he's the Geek Who Can Speak," sure enough the other person says, "Oh yeah, I know who you mean."

Supply

Afford, deliver, dispense, endow, equip, fulfill, furnished, give, grant, issue, outfit, provide, stock

Support

Verbs: Advocate, aid, approve, assist, back, bolster, champion, encourage, endorse, fund, promote, reinforce, shoulder, sponsor, sustain, uphold

Systematize

Arrange, design, devise, establish, frame, institute, methodize, order, organize, plan, regulated, standardize

Quotes From The Queen

Target companies: These are companies or organizations where you'd love to work. You develop this list by doing research and matching to your values and goals what you learn about companies. Those that fit you end up on the list. Next step: networking your way into a select few of these companies. For more on this topic, see *How to Network Your Way Into a Company* by Joanne Meehl at:

www.theresumequeen.com/downloadables.htm

T

Tabulate
Arrange, catalogue, categorize, chart, classify, codify, count, formulate, index, inventory, list, order, record, register

Tailor
Accommodate, adapt, adjust, alter, conform, convert, fashion, modify, mold, shape, style, trim

Teach
Advise, coach, demonstrate, direct, educate, explain, guide, illustrate, inform, instruct, prepare, ready, school, train, tutor

Tend
Administer, attend, control, cultivate, direct, follow, foster, guard, handle, maintain, manage, mind, minister, oversee, supervise, watch

Terminate
Abort, cancel, cease, close, complete, conclude, culminate, discharge, discontinue, dismiss, dissolve, drop, eliminate, end, expire, finish, leave, resign, stop

Total
Verbs: Add, calculate, compute, count, figure, summate, tally

Nouns: Amount, sum, tally

Trace
Follow, search, track, watch

Track
Chase, follow, hunt, observe, pursue, trace, trail

Quotes From The Queen

I could have added the affected *utilize* but, preferring the power of simplicity, I don't like the word because it uses three syllables when *use* uses one. So use *use* instead.

Trade
Verbs: Bargain, barter, deal, exchange, negotiate, substitute, swap

Nouns: Art, avocation, business, craft, line, occupation, position, profession, skill, vocation

Train(ed)
Verbs: Coach, cultivate, develop, direct, educate, equip, guide, groom, hone, instruct, practice, prepare, prime, school, season, shape, taught, tutor

Adjectives: Accomplished, adept, competent, disciplined, educated, inform, proficient, qualified, schooled, skilled

Transfer
Assign, change, convey, delegate, dispatch, dispense, hand, move, reassign, relegate, relocate, remove, restation, send, shift, transplant

Transform
Alter, change, convert, metamorphose, modify, mold, reconstruct, revamp, switch, vary

Translate
Construe, decipher, decode, elucidate, explain, interpret, paraphrase, transcribe, turn

Transport
Bring, carry, convey, fare, ferry, move, send, shift, ship, truck

Trim
Clip, crop, curtail, cut, decrease, lessen, minify, pare, reduce, shave, shorten, tailor, truncate

Triple
Increase, multiply, threefold, thrice, triad, trio

Quotes From The Queen

Value: Your value (V Factor) is measured in three ways. Not everyone can *score* in all three ways. It's great if you can, but some occupations lend themselves to one over the others. These are:

1. By how you save or make money. A successful salesperson *makes* money for a company; an accountant *saves* money.

2. By how you *save* or *make* time. Now you really can't do either of those things with time, but you can *create* time for another person by, for example, off-loading some work from their work load. A technical writer who takes on a task that frees up an engineer is someone who's proving their value to everyone around them.

3. By solving problems. The person who says *"I'll take care of that,"* and then *does* take care of it, becomes valuable to everyone around them.

During a job search, all your communications with a potential employer should address at least one of these. Your *value* is what gets you hired.

U

Uncover
Bare, disclose, discover, display, divulge, expose, impart, reveal, show, uncover, unearth, unmask, unveil

Undertake
Attempt, begin, commence, contract, endeavor, engage, initiate, launch, shoulder, start, try, venture, volunteer

Unify
Affiliate, ally, amalgamate, blend, combine, compound, concert, consolidate, harmonize, integrate, join, merge, mingle, mix, unite

Unravel
Decipher, disentangle, figure, separate, solve, unfold, undo, unscramble

Update
Bring up to date: Amend, modernize, modify, refresh, rejuvenate, renew, restore, revise

Impart knowledge: Advise, brief, counsel, explain, familiarize, inform, report

Use
Accept, adopt, apply, employ, exercise, operate, practice, utilize

Quotes From The Queen

Leave a *voice mail* that will get results. If you're following up after sending a resume, a good voice mail restates your value: *"Hi, this is John Jones, the tech support manager who reduces response time by 25%, calling to follow up on the resume I sent two weeks ago."* That kind of message gets a better response than *"I'm following up on the resume I sent,"* all by itself.

V

Vacate
Abandon, abdicate, abjure, clear, depart, discharge, empty, leave, relinquish

Various
Assorted, changing, different, distinctive, diverse, individual, multiple, numerous varied

Verify
Attest, authenticate, certify, check, confirm, establish, guarantee, prove, substantiate, test, validate

Quotes From The Queen

Today's job search is vastly different than it was a generation ago. It used to be that employees were rewarded for loyalty with the security of lifelong jobs. They worked their way up a ladder. Today, the job search is more like climbing a rock wall: sometimes you go up, sometimes sideways, and sometimes even down a step to go up five.

W

Weigh
Analyze, appraise, balance, consider, contemplate, deliberate, estimate, evaluate, examine, measure, ponder, reflect, study

Widen
Augment, broaden, enlarge, expand, extend, grow, increase, multiply, spread, stretch

Win
Achieve, acquire, attain, conquer, earn, gain, got, net, overcome, prevail, reach, realize, secure, succeed

Withdraw
Abjure, disengage, leave, recant, recede, remove, renounce, rescind, retire, retract, retreat

Withstand
Bear, brave, confront, endure, face, hold, oppose, resist, stand, take, tolerate, traverse

Work
Commission, conduct, employ, function, labor, operate, practice, perform, specialize, strive, travail

Write
Author, compose, correspond, create, draft, formulate, note, pen, pencil, publish, record, transcribe

About the Author

Joanne Meehl is a career transition management consultant with clients all over the US and beyond. "What drives me is the belief that since we each work for more than one-third of our waking hours, we should be satisfied with what we do. Our lives are fleeting and the time we have is precious. It's my calling that I help people find out what their best role in life should be."

In graduate school, Joanne had an internship in a college counseling center and then landed a job in a community college near Boston. She thought she would become the next Carl Rogers. However, the students' concerns were all about their careers. She loved the work and never looked back. Today she works with professionals of all ages who don't just want a new job; they want a satisfying career.

Joanne's own career detours, from computer software/hardware sales to technical writing, gave her expertise that she still applies to her work today. And life's tough surprises — lightning striking her house and setting it on fire, cancer, and divorce . . . all in four years — were humbling. They reinforced her beliefs in the value of friendship and in taking adversity and turning it into resolve.

Joanne is also a widely published essay writer whose work has appeared in *The Washington Post, The Boston Globe,* and elsewhere.

She has two stepsons, and lives in rural Massachusetts with her husband, their dog, and two cats. For more information, visit her website, www.TheResumeQueen.com.